5-MINUTE MORNING MAGIC

Daily Self-Talk for Creating the Life of Your Dreams

MARYSE CARDIN

CASTLE POINT BOOKS
NEW YORK

This morning magic
belongs to:

_____

I RISE
**WITH
THE SUN
AND MY
WORDS**

START THE DAY OFF ON THE RIGHT FOOT BY CHANGING THE WAY YOU TALK TO YOURSELF.

The inner voice we all have in our heads can either propel us to happiness and prosperity or compel us to repeat the same mistakes over and over. Only you can choose your course and take a bold step toward the life of your dreams! What you say to yourself in the morning lets your head, heart, and spirit know where you're going and what your focus needs to be to get there. That's the power of self-talk.

It's simple to get started with *5-Minute Morning Magic*. As you sip your coffee or tea, you can also drink in uplifting and energizing self-talk. It's a boost that lasts a lot longer than caffeine! Embrace the messages and reflective questions in the order they appear in the book, or flip the book open and let the universe lead you to a daily focus. Take it one message a day, or repeat your favorite inspiration over several mornings. This is your own joyful journey. No matter where you land, you'll find positive words to help you breathe out your doubts and breathe in calm confidence for both the day ahead and your greater life journey.

In just 5 minutes a day, you can summon strength, passion, and purpose. Get ready for the magic to rise from within!

I AM IN
CONTROL

SELF-TALK IS WITHIN MY CONTROL. Like a DJ who compiles a playlist, I intentionally choose my inner music. I speak to myself with love, encouragement, gentleness, and humor. Inner words hold power to direct my day and carry even farther to steer my life. No matter what happens, I am in control of how I respond—both in the world and within myself. I become aware of my inner conversation. When I notice that my inner critic won't stop the running commentary, I deliberately replace it with a voice that is accepting and positive.

⊕ ⊕ ⊕ ⊕ ⊕

Do I speak to myself like I am someone who matters to me?

What powerful things will I say to myself today?

How will those words lead my feelings and my actions?

⊕ ⊕ ⊕ ⊕ ⊕

I STAY
**OPEN TO
POSSIBILITY**

**NO MORE SLAMMING DOORS WHEN I DON'T
EVEN KNOW WHAT'S ON THE OTHER SIDE!**
My heart is ready to take risks and open to all the
good that life offers: love, beauty, prosperity, health,
discovery, and connection. I am ready to see and say
yes to so many opportunities custom-made for me.
I receive with gratitude and grace compliments that
point me to my strengths. I accept invitations to life's
limitless adventures. I welcome wisdom—for the day
and for life—shared with me. I breathe in all that is
possible in this moment and all the gifts that are still
to come.

* * * * *

*What door that I've closed in the past
could I reopen right now?*

*What new doors do I see myself opening
in the near future?*

*What beautiful moments of possibility
are in store for me today?*

* * * * *

I NO LONGER BUY INTO THE CONSTANT RUSH, THE MAD DASH, AND THE SELF-IMPOSED DEADLINES. I stop pushing myself to the point where I cannot find satisfaction. Now, I breathe deeply and gently as I slow down to my own time; real time that is sustainable and meaningful. Many wonderful things in life come together slowly, like growing up, healing, or cooking a meal from scratch. I allow the time and space needed for answers to come to my questions and for paths to clear to my dreams. I'm not stopping, but I am slowing to a pace that makes sense to get me where I want to go.

● ● ● ● ●

How will I pause my to-do list and give my attention to my dreams?

How can I create space in my schedule and settings for quiet processing?

What will bring me true satisfaction at the end of the day?

● ● ● ● ●

I HOLD
CALM
WITHIN

WHEN MY NERVOUS SYSTEM IS OVERWHELMED, WIRED, OR ANXIOUS, I HOLD THE POWER TO HELP IT CALM DOWN. I bring myself back into balance with calming tools—maybe meditation, a hot bath, deep breathing, talking to a friend, a nature walk, or reading a favorite book. I know what works for me if I really listen to and connect with myself. I reach for the healthful benefits of soothing versus the false promises of numbing. As I relax, I am reunited with my real self, the one who feels at ease once the nervous energy is lifted. I am not my anxiety or worry. I can acknowledge these feelings and then show them the door.

● ● ● ● ●

*What calming tool will
I turn to today?*

*How will I be ready to listen
for what I need?*

*How can I keep the real me
shining through?*

● ● ● ● ●

I AM
ONE OF A KIND

MY DESIGN IS EXCEPTIONAL. I DON'T QUESTION WHY I'M DIFFERENT FROM THE CROWD. Instead, I love and honor all the qualities that make me remarkable. I see and experience the world in my own way. This is beneficial for me and the world. I don't expect to be understood by everybody. I won't waste my time and energy trying to fit in or to be someone else. The world needs me just as I am. I am always enough and never too much. I soar when I celebrate my glorious, unconventional nature.

* * * * *

What's one remarkable quality I will share with the world today?

In what situation could this quality be life-changing for me and others?

How will I feel at the end of a day lived as the true me?

* * * * *

I DISCOVER MOMENTS OF FRESH ENERGY IN EVERY DAY, even when I need to intentionally build them into my schedule. I find reasons to feel good, to be amused, and to laugh. I am a magnet for friends who are positive and playful too. As I relax my tight grip on things, I feel myself free to experience beautiful moments and connections and to follow my dreams. I choose not to take myself too seriously, even as I care deeply and look for ways to grow. It's a happy balance that fuels my mind, body, and spirit.

* * * * *

*What can I depend on to bring
me joy every day?*

*Where are new places I can seek
playful experiences?*

*Where will my positive energy and
free spirit carry me today?*

* * * * *

I AM
**POWERFULLY
PRESENT**

MY PRESENCE IS MEANINGFUL IN MY LIFE AND THE LIVES OF OTHERS. When I am with someone, I give them all my attention. I want the people in my life to know that they are important to me. I give this full attention to myself too. I put down my phone and bring my awareness to myself. I put my hand on my heart to gain a deeper connection and to show myself that I am all in, with no distractions. I am aware and take notice of what's going on inside and all around me. I am fully and happily here.

● ● ● ● ●

Can I be present right now, bringing my full attention to myself?

What do I notice inside me as I put my hand on my heart for a deeper connection?

What do I notice all around me?

● ● ● ● ●

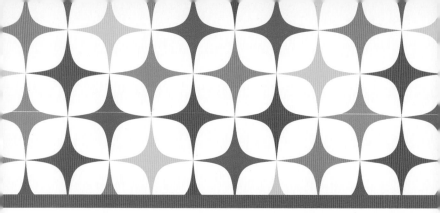

I WELCOME
HELP WITH
GRATITUDE

I PUSH ASIDE ANY NOTION THAT I MUST FIND WHAT I NEED AND WANT ALL ON MY OWN.
There's no prize for receiving the least amount of help. Whether it's a simple hand to get through a daily task or a boost that will alter the rest of my life, I welcome assistance in all its pure and positive forms. If my request for help is refused, I don't take it personally but immediately look to new sources. I will find compassionate people who can offer what I need. When I receive their assistance, I am filled with gratitude for the goodness and love that comes my way.

⬧ ⬧ ⬧ ⬧ ⬧

Have I reached a point where help is needed to create the life I want?

Who has the wisdom and tools to help me?

Do I have any resistance to asking for help, and where does that resistance come from?

⬧ ⬧ ⬧ ⬧ ⬧

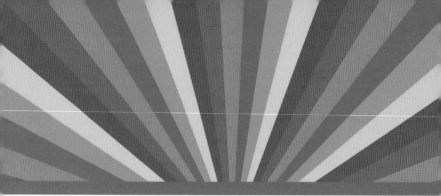

I AM
BEAUTIFUL

I SHINE IN ALL THE GLORY OF MY NATURAL BEAUTY. I smile and wink at the exquisite, magical me I see in the mirror. No matter what season of life I am in, I appreciate that my beauty is ageless, not dependent on conventions and fashions. I dress and accentuate my beauty in all kinds of ways for the sheer pleasure of celebrating my own splendor and uniqueness. I generously compliment myself like I do my favorite people. Beauty is in the eyes of the beholder, and I turn this loving vision to my inner and outer gorgeousness.

● ● ● ● ●

*How will I let my beauty
shine today?*

*What parts of myself do
I find beautiful?*

What makes me feel gorgeous?

● ● ● ● ●

I KNOW
WHEN TO
WALK
AWAY

SOME THINGS NEED TO END TO CLEAR SPACE FOR OTHERS TO BEGIN. I am willing to leave behind relationships and situations that are toxic or unsupportive. It is my responsibility and my right to care for myself. Breakups and endings are not necessarily failures— I accept that people change and situations can run their course. I believe in honorable endings as I gather the remains that are precious and let go of the rest. When people vanish from my life, I grieve, give thanks for shared experiences, and bid them farewell. I walk away when it's necessary with my head held high, looking straight into the future with a courageous heart.

* * * * *

Would I benefit from leaving someone or something behind right now?

What would it look like to have an honorable ending?

Is there someone from the past to whom I can show gratitude in my heart and finally find release?

* * * * *

I START
AGAIN

EVERY DAY IS A FRESH OPPORTUNITY TO GET IT RIGHT. I keep the porch light on for myself and never give up. There is no end to the chances I allow myself. If I fail or fall, I go back to the basics and start again when I'm ready. I am never too late, too old, or too lost to find my way to what is truly me, truly mine. I can choose a fresh start right this very moment— whether I dive in or take a gentle half step in the right direction. I know that one day I will reach and embrace the understanding that has eluded me until now.

＊ ＊ ＊ ＊ ＊

*In what area of my life do
I need a fresh start?*

*Am I truly committed to giving myself
as many chances as I may need?*

*What can I do today that will be the
first step to a second chance?*

＊ ＊ ＊ ＊ ＊

I LIVE
**LIFE TO THE
FULLEST**

I CELEBRATE THE GIFT OF LIFE I HAVE BEEN GIVEN. Every moment's chance to feel alive within my body and my spirit is not squandered on me. What sparks that feeling is uniquely mine to discover and pursue. I follow my passions to make the most of every day. I am fully awake to life's beauty and mindful of the opportunities that come my way. I want to experience the entirety that life has to offer. When I think about all of the possibilities, energy courses through me. I could even say that life is living in me.

· · · · ·

*Am I living my life to
its fullest?*

*How can I take advantage of what's
possible for me today?*

*What feels most alive and
exciting to me?*

· · · · ·

I RECOGNIZE THE POWER IN BEING MY OWN BEST FRIEND. A best friend listens, compliments, delights in simple presence, and answers calls to help or to have fun. I speak to myself like I am someone whom I love and cherish. I take my dreams seriously. I am fully committed to my well-being. I make dates with myself for the sheer joy of being with someone who cares deeply about me. And when I get a glimpse of my gorgeous and brave face in the mirror, I greet that special person with the kindness, warmth, and respect a friend is worthy of receiving.

· · · · ·

How will I show myself that I am my own best friend today?

What is important to me in friendship?

How will I greet myself in the mirror?

· · · · ·

I FACE
MY FEARS

FEAR HAS VALID INFORMATION TO SHARE WITH ME. I remember that fear is in service to me and is there to be helpful. It's part of my natural makeup that enables me to be wise, to be strategic, to stop, or to get away. Fear, however, is not a force that needs to paralyze me and plague me forever. I listen for what fear is trying to tell me and then take measures to quiet my fear. When I stop running from my fears and face them, they lighten, like opening a window in a dark, stuffy room.

⊕ ⊕ ⊕ ⊕ ⊕

Is fear keeping me from doing anything I really want to do?

What scares me right now?

What would it look like to be scared but do what I desire anyway?

⊕ ⊕ ⊕ ⊕ ⊕

I AM
LUMINOUS

I LET MY OWN LIGHT SHINE BRIGHTLY. I am no longer an accomplice to the dimming of it. In fact, I look for ways to increase the light I offer myself and the world around me. If someone is uncomfortable with how bright I am, I invite them to look away. I am at my most luminous when I'm my authentic self, radiating my own unique energy and joy. I light the way for my own possibilities. My radiance also brightens the hearts and lives of those who encounter it. Brilliance in all its forms enters my life because like attracts like.

* * * * *

*How will I let myself
shine today?*

*Are there ways in which I have
been dimming my light?*

*How can I increase my
own luminosity?*

* * * * *

I SET
A CLEAR
INTENTION

AN INTENTION IS MY VERY OWN GPS TO MY HEART'S DESIRE. It guides my way and informs my decisions. It helps all of me align in the direction I am headed. I'm not interested in bobbing around aimlessly. I set an intense intention about what I want, who I want to be, and how I want to live. No worries if I'm not sure how to get there. That knowledge will absolutely come with time. What's important is that I know where I'm headed. The rest of my life starts this very instant. Watch me set a course for it.

● ● ● ● ●

What is my intention for this new day?

How clear am I about my intentions?

How do I really want to live?

● ● ● ● ●

I RESERVE TIME FOR ME. I CAREFULLY GUARD MY SLEEPING HOURS. They are not what I cut out on busy days, when I'm most in need of their restorative powers. I treat myself to naps and to time for relaxation. I unplug, put away my screens, and honor my need for time-outs. My body, mind, and spirit deserve time to recharge and grow even stronger and more resilient. I give myself a chance to rejuvenate instead of fitting just one more task into my day. I design time to rest so that I am ready and capable to live my best life every day.

* * * * *

*When will I take time
to rest today?*

*Am I getting all the
sleep I need?*

*Beyond sleep, what makes
me feel well rested?*

* * * * *

I CAN
SAY NO

I SET COMPASSIONATE BOUNDARIES. Knowing how to say no is a skill as necessary as walking. If someone gets mad at me because I said no, it doesn't mean I should have said yes. If it's not for me, or I'm overextended, I can say no and still be compassionate, and still love. It's not always easy to say no, and I am proud of myself when I do. I have matured out of the need to be seen as nice by saying yes when I don't mean it. Sometimes, out of self-love, I even say no to myself because I need to set my own limits.

* * * * *

Is there someone I need to say no to today?

Am I clear on my own healthy boundaries?

Is there something I've said yes to recently when my true answer was no?

* * * * *

I CAN
SAY YES

WHEN I HEAR A RESOUNDING *YES* INSIDE, I GO FOR IT. I let myself be happy. I overcome my own resistance to something new that may scare me. It can be something for my highest good or a whimsy that my heart desires. I know what yes feels like inside me—the emotional and physical sensations that arise. I don't have to justify my yes to anyone or even fully understand it myself. Yes means yes! I know what is right and true for me in the moment, and I'm always allowed to change my mind and course as needed. The biggest yes I give is to my own power.

● ● ● ● ●

*What do I want to say
yes to today?*

*Is there something in
my life that I have been too
scared to say yes to?*

*Can I touch base deep within me
to feel what is calling me?*

● ● ● ● ●

I TREASURE
MY WISDOM AND INSIGHT

**MY WISDOM IS DEEP-ROOTED AND HAS
PRACTICAL APPLICATIONS.** I have a knowing that
I tap into before speaking or acting. Only fools jump
in without taking counsel with their wisdom. I am a
discerning soul and seek insight before making decisions.
I show good judgment and shrewd understanding. I tell
people that I'll get back to them after I've had time to
reflect. My sensibility guides me. I deepen my wisdom
by asking questions and listening, sitting quietly in
contemplation, and reading.

⊕ ⊕ ⊕ ⊕ ⊕

*How will I lead with my
wisdom today?*

*What have I done lately to
increase my wisdom?*

*Do I tap into my inner knowledge
before speaking or acting?*

⊕ ⊕ ⊕ ⊕ ⊕

I FORGIVE
AND FIND
FREEDOM

FORGIVENESS OPENS THE DOOR TO AN EXPANDED FUTURE FOR ME. I choose to forgive so I have the freedom to walk a new path, one that doesn't keep me entangled with a person or situation. I have the wisdom to know that forgiveness is not condoning. Forgiveness is an act of healing. I forgive because I am more in love with the possibilities of my future than I am attached to the pain in my past. I shine this light of mercy on myself as well. I learn wisely from mistakes and renew my life by forgiving myself. I don't turn my back on myself by withholding forgiveness.

⬤ ⬤ ⬤ ⬤ ⬤

*Is there someone
(even myself) whom I feel
ready to forgive today?*

*Am I hanging on to something
painful from my past?*

*How does forgiveness
benefit me?*

⬤ ⬤ ⬤ ⬤ ⬤

I AM
REFLECTIVE

I EXAMINE MY LIFE ON A REGULAR BASIS— NOT JUST WHEN I FEEL A CRISIS COMING ON.

I don't live blindly, fearing introspection. I want to be in an intimate relationship with my life. I want to know what it means to me. My waters run deep and I need space to dive for discovery and resurface with answers. I long for contemplative time after my focus has been outbound. If someone shares something with me, I may come back to them after I've sat with it. I refuse to be rushed into anything when I feel ambiguity. I take the time I need to reach thoughtful decisions that are right for me.

· · · · ·

*What needs examining in
my life today?*

*Do I take enough time
to contemplate?*

Do I rush into decisions?

· · · · ·

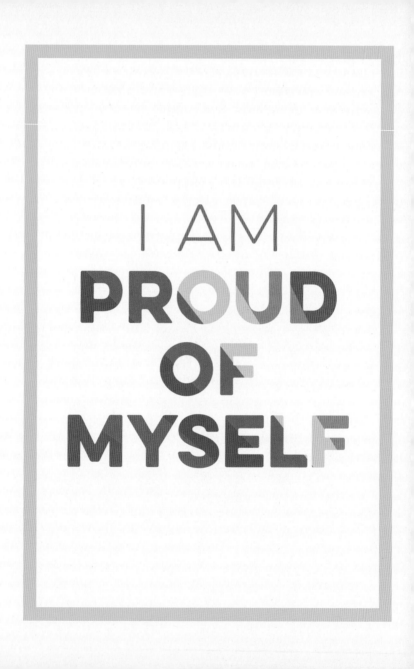

I VALUE MYSELF. I HAVE EARNED MY OWN RESPECT OVER TIME BY COMMITTING TO MY LIFE PRIORITIES. I have self-gratitude for all the efforts I have made and the hard work I have put in. I admire my determination. I am proud of my successes and the lessons I have learned. Every day I keep walking in the direction of my right life, growing, learning, and evolving. It's an honor to lead this life. I determine my own worth. It's an inside job that cannot be given or taken away by anyone else.

* * * * *

*In what areas of my life am
I most proud of myself?*

*Do I take time to acknowledge all
the efforts I have made?*

*What can I do today to show
myself appreciation?*

* * * * *

I LOVE
MYSELF
WHOLLY

I TAKE EVERY OPPORTUNITY TO SHOW MYSELF WITH MY WORDS AND WITH MY ACTIONS THAT I AM LOVED UNCONDITIONALLY. Self-love is a way of life for me as I open my heart to myself. I am able to embrace my entirety—what I'm proud of and what makes me cringe or want to hide. No more withholding my love because I think I'm not perfect or because I've made mistakes. All of me is deserving of my gentle care, no matter how I perceive the outcomes of my choices within any particular day. My love is a constant, and my heart is a home to which I can always return.

* * * * *

*In what ways will I show
myself love today?*

*What do I love about
myself?*

*How important is
self-love to me?*

* * * * *

I DEFINE
**SUCCESS
FOR
MYSELF**

I AM SUCCESSFUL ON MY OWN TERMS. I have the sovereignty to write my very own success story based on my very own principles. A good life is not about how anything looks to outsiders or about their approval. I believe thoroughly in my strength and ability to create a successful life that is uniquely mine. I know what I want and why I want it, and I put my intention, faith, and energy on its attainment. I wake up each morning happy for a new day, enjoying my life and finding purpose.

* * * * *

How do I measure success in my own life?

Am I following my own standards or those of society?

What are my favorite memories of achieving success?

* * * * *

I AM
RESILIENT

WHEN I LOOK BACK AT WHERE I'VE BEEN AND HOW FAR I'VE COME, I SEE THAT I AM CAPABLE of way more than I ever would have thought possible. I have incredible endurance. I persevere through adverse times. I am my own bedrock, solid and steady. I am solidly in for the duration. I am encouraged by my own track record of showing persistence until I have triumphed. I keep going step by step with compassion for myself until I succeed. I have faith in my abilities, my strength, my determination, and my resilience. I come back from setbacks and rebound, rally, and recover. I stand again, reinvigorated.

⬤ ⬤ ⬤ ⬤ ⬤

*What will necessitate
endurance today?*

*In what ways have I shown
resilience in the past?*

*Can I trust myself to show this
same kind of resilience now?*

⬤ ⬤ ⬤ ⬤ ⬤

I TRUST
IN LIFE

I TRUST THE NEXT STEP WILL BE APPARENT WHEN THE TIME IS RIGHT, in the same way that my headlights illuminate the road right ahead of me in the blackest of nights. I trust myself fully, and I know that I have my highest interest at heart. I trust others to play the role they are meant to in my life. I trust life to care for my well-being and to open doors. I trust the universe to cocreate with me. It's not all riding on my shoulders. Trusting doesn't mean that I don't question or make choices thoughtfully. It means that I know there's a big picture. The burden to have it all figured out lifts, so I can relax into a more enjoyable life.

⬤ ⬤ ⬤ ⬤ ⬤

How can I show trust in myself today?

How can I show trust in the bigger picture of my life today?

Do I tell myself that it will all work out?

⬤ ⬤ ⬤ ⬤ ⬤

I AM
STRONG

**MY STRENGTH IS ROOTED DEEP WITHIN ME;
IT IS NOT A SHALLOW SURFACE STRENGTH.**
It shows up in my will, my self-knowledge, my spirit,
my body, my mind, and my endurance through days
that go my way and days that don't. I am solid, fierce,
and powerful. I am unsinkable. There is no reason to
ever think of myself as not strong enough because
I can always make the decision to get stronger in
whatever areas I need. There are limitless ways I can
increase my physical, emotional, and spiritual strength
to benefit myself and the world around me. I have what
it takes. All I need to do is set my intention and begin.

· · · · ·

*What will I put my strength
in service to today?*

*Do I have any false beliefs that
I am not strong enough?*

*How can I become stronger physically,
emotionally, and spiritually?*

· · · · ·

I THRIVE IN
SIMPLICITY

I KNOW THAT HAPPINESS IS NOT FOUND IN A BOX AND THAT WHAT REALLY MAKES ME HAPPY IS FREE: chatting with a friend, spending time in nature, or sipping a hot drink as the sun shines through the window. I seek simple joys to fill my life. I am not interested in complicated stories or drama. I value clarity in words and actions. There is a beauty in simplicity that appeals greatly to me and makes me feel at peace. I surround myself with objects that make me smile or that are helpful. I have no use for excess. I don't really need very much to be happy.

● ● ● ● ●

What can I do today to make my life simpler?

In what ways do I tend to complicate my life?

What is very simple and clear for me?

● ● ● ● ●

I DO NOT REVOLVE AROUND ANYONE ELSE AS THOUGH THEY ARE THE SUN. I am the center of my own life, and I prioritize my well-being. It is from a strong center that I interact with others and go forth into the world. My feet are solidly planted in this foundation. I return again and again to this center as it is my source of strength. It's here that I get recharged to go back and immerse myself in the world and all its possibilities. I cannot control anyone else or their actions, but I can choose how I live my life—according to my authentic self and following my heart's callings.

● ● ● ● ●

*Am I living like I am my
own center?*

*Have I prioritized
my needs?*

*Have I given away so much
of my power to someone that I am
revolving around them?*

● ● ● ● ●

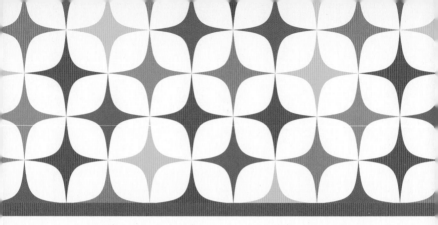

I BELIEVE
IN MAGIC

EVERYWHERE I GO I CAN SEE THE WONDERS THAT LIFE HAS TO OFFER. I know that the seemingly impossible is, in fact, extremely possible. I am ready to defy the odds and reap the rewards. It all starts with my mindset. When I expect big things (even what some might call miracles), my wildest dreams manifest right before my eyes. Doors open and joy appears as if the events were fated all along. I wake up each day feeling enchanted and ready to dance with the mystery that is my life. Magic is possible. Magic is within me. I believe I can make anything happen.

⬤ ⬤ ⬤ ⬤ ⬤

What miracle making is possible today?

What do I believe will happen even if the odds are slim?

What is my wildest dream?

⬤ ⬤ ⬤ ⬤ ⬤

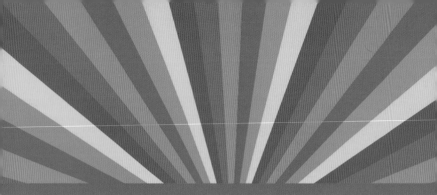

I LIVE WITH
COMPASSION

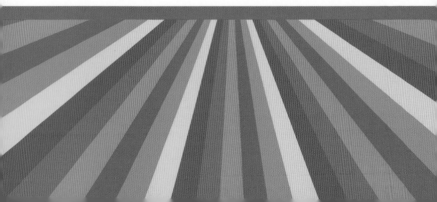

IT IS THROUGH THE LENS OF COMPASSION THAT I PARTICIPATE IN THIS WORLD. My compassionate nature extends to all players in any situation. I offer my empathy freely instead of judging or compulsively overhelping. I embody self-compassion too, especially when I have failed to meet my own moral standards or have made a mistake. I enjoy all the benefits that a compassionate state brings, such as better health and more inner calm.

◉ ◉ ◉ ◉ ◉

Is there a situation in my life that can use way more compassion today?

Do I ever feel a compulsion to overhelp instead of simply giving my compassion?

How do I treat myself when I've made a mistake or have failed in some way?

◉ ◉ ◉ ◉ ◉

I HONOR
SEASONS

I AM FULLY AWARE THAT THERE IS A SEASON FOR EVERYTHING. I celebrate what's possible in any given moment. I experience the beauty of seasonal gifts in nature and in my life. There is a cycle and a divine timing to all that's alive. I dance in the vibrancy and sunlight of summer and know that certain good things come to fruition in winter's darkness. I gratefully receive what's on offer in this current season and wait patiently, and with great faith, for the bounty of other seasons to follow. Each will come at just the right time and bring what's needed.

●　●　●　●　●

What is something that I take delight in during this season?

What's a benefit of being in this season of my life?

What do I look forward to?

●　●　●　●　●

I AM
BRAVE

I AM CAPABLE OF GREAT ACTS OF BRAVERY, ON BEHALF OF MYSELF AND OTHERS. I can take bold steps in new directions. I keep going when I feel it to be true and right, even when facing the unknown. My courage and my fear sometimes coexist, mutually unexclusive. I find strength in following the lead of my heart. I see adversity and disquieting life events as opportunities to build that big heart and my courage muscles. Being brave brings new life into motion and opens doors. My most daring move is courageously claiming the life of my dreams that is mine to have.

* * * * *

In what areas of my life do I need to show courage?

How have I shown courage in the past?

What act of bravery will I carry out today?

* * * * *

SELF-CARE IS A PRIORITY IN MY LIFE. I take care of my body with rest, movement, and nourishing foods. I take care of my mind with meditation, relaxation, and learning. I take care of my spirit with contemplation or prayer and time spent in community that is meaningful to me. I take care of my whole self by taking time and space to rejuvenate. When the care I need is beyond what I can do on my own, I recognize that fact and reach out for help. Each time I give myself care I'm saying, "You are important to me. You are loved."

* * * * *

*How will I take care of
myself today?*

*What part of me is most in need
of my attention?*

*What is my favorite way
to rejuvenate?*

* * * * *

I AM
ANCHORED

I FEEL MY FEET ON THE SOLID GROUND AND I BREATHE SLOWLY, DEEPLY, IN AND OUT.
In and out. This mindfulness practice anchors me in the present moment. There is so much happening right this second. I only need to take notice and be present to appreciate it. My life can only be lived in the now. The past is finished, and the future is yet to come. What I do have is the present and I mindfully inhabit it, taking each moment and day as it comes and embracing all the good possible.

*   *   *   *   *

Can I take a moment right now to breathe slowly and anchor myself in the present?

Can I feel my two feet planted solidly on the ground?

What are my favorite mindfulness practices?

*   *   *   *   *

I KNOW
MY
WORTH

MY SELF-ESTEEM TRANSCENDS THE CHALLENGES I FACE AND THE OPINIONS OF OTHERS. I am more important than my problems. I may question my decisions and actions, but I don't put my worth into question. I feel deep affection for the person that I am, and I respect the efforts that I make. Under no circumstances do I neglect or abuse myself by engaging in negative self-talk, ignoring self-care, or putting everyone else ahead of me. I protect and stand up for myself, showing up stronger with every day.

● ● ● ● ●

*Do I speak to myself
with respect?*

*How could I show myself even
more consideration?*

*Are there any problems I have allowed
to overshadow my worth?*

● ● ● ● ●

I AM
PERFECTLY
WHOLE

I AM NOT A FIXER-UPPER IN CONSTANT NEED OF RENOVATION. I am complete and whole just the way I already am. I am enough. There is nothing to chase. I am not a half person in need of someone else to be complete. All parts of me come into balance and unity as I drop the false belief that I am not good enough or lacking in some way. I am utterly and perfectly intact no matter what has happened in my life until now. I can relax in the magnificent wholeness into which I was born.

· · · · ·

*Do I realize I am perfectly whole
just the way I am right now?*

*What does it mean to be
a complete person?*

*How will I acknowledge and celebrate
my wholeness today?*

· · · · ·

I RELEASE
THE PAST

THERE IS NOTHING THAT I NEED TO HANG ON TO. I don't long for what's no longer here, nor do I chase ghosts. The more I let go of what's behind me, the more I welcome space for change and new beginnings. I easily learn what I need to learn from my past and happily move on. There's so much awaiting me. I keep happy and loving memories close to my heart and release the rest with gratitude. I regularly declutter objects from my home and old beliefs from my inner self. There is very little that is essential to my happiness going forward. What a freeing thought that is!

● ● ● ● ●

What have I been hanging on to?

What can I joyfully release from my past today?

Is it time to declutter my inner self of old beliefs or my home of old objects?

● ● ● ● ●

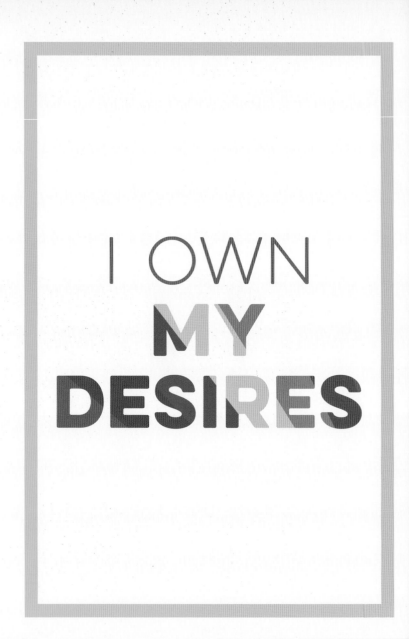

I DESIRE A LIFE FILLED WITH PASSION, ADVENTURE, MEANINGFUL WORK, GROWTH, JOY, PEACE, INTIMACY, LOVE, AND FRIENDSHIP. I know that whatever I desire is a natural expression of who I am. It may be a lighthearted whimsy or a lifelong dream that I am determined to manifest. My desires naturally evolve as I change. Sometimes I am surprised by the intensity of a yearning. It's as though whatever I seek is seeking me. I listen to my heart's longings, and I acknowledge what it wants. There is a raw and precious truth to my desires. I don't deny or belittle them. They have a place in my life that I can determine. I invite my desires to come forth into my consciousness.

● ● ● ● ●

What have I desired in the past that I had the good fortune to receive?

Do I have a desire that I can barely acknowledge even to myself?

What does my heart want today?

● ● ● ● ●

I AM
GRATEFUL

I RECOGNIZE AND GIVE THANKS FOR THE BIG AND SMALL BLESSINGS IN MY LIFE. I take time to contemplate the ways in which my life works, and what I have been offered. I have so many reasons to be grateful and to feel lucky. I am appreciative of both what I've received in the past and what's to come. I am humbled by all the good that surrounds me each day. I find joy in life's tiny benefits, like clean sheets, and in momentous gifts, like love in all forms. Some of the simplest yet most powerful words I can utter are *thank you.*

* * * * *

*What am I particularly grateful
for at this moment?*

How does gratitude elevate me?

*Can something that I once
saw as a negative now be seen
as a blessing?*

* * * * *

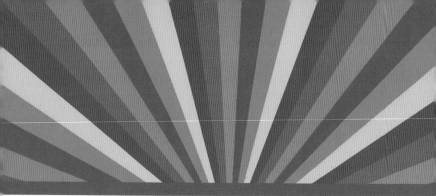

I NURTURE
FRIENDSHIPS

I CELEBRATE MY FRIENDSHIPS AND SEEK WAYS TO BE A GOOD, SUPPORTIVE FRIEND. I value my true-blue friends who see me through thick and thin and make my life richer. I recognize their kindness, loyalty, and companionship. I show my friends my truth so they can know and appreciate the real me. I feel seen and appreciated by them. Some friends are in my life forever, while others come in for a shorter though no less meaningful stint. I devotedly keep them close and let them know what they mean to me.

* * * * *

How can I be a better friend?

Which people have seen me through thick and thin?

Is there anyone in my life with whom I would like to strengthen my friendship?

* * * * *

I KNOW
WHO I AM

THERE IS NOTHING ABOUT ME THAT I AM AFRAID OF KNOWING. Self-knowledge empowers me. It helps me make decisions and know whether something is or isn't for me. I know my qualities, and where I shine. I am also intimately acquainted with my darker characteristics. Both are an integral part of me. I know my own mind and heart as I check in with them regularly. I set free my true voice and fiercely show up as me. I honor and love the authentic me.

● ● ● ● ●

How deep is my self-knowledge?

What are some of my strengths?

Can I accept that I have both strengths and darker characteristics, making me a healthy and whole person?

● ● ● ● ●

I GENEROUSLY GIVE OUT SOME OF THE GOOD STUFF THAT I HAVE. I share my time, my space, my good fortune, my ideas, my talent, my presence. I give these consciously, wisely without expectation, purely out of love. I know how precious these contributions are. I am aware of the abundance with which I've been gifted, and I share it with a light heart. There is nothing I need to hoard because abundance flows to me, through me to others, and back again full circle. I easily give and I easily receive.

◉ ◉ ◉ ◉ ◉

*In what areas do I feel like
I have an abundance?*

What will I share today?

*In what ways have others been
generous with me?*

◉ ◉ ◉ ◉ ◉

I AM
DESERVING

I DESERVE AND GIVE MYSELF THE GOOD THINGS I GIVE OTHERS—INCLUDING KIND WORDS, LOVE, TIME, AND THE BENEFIT OF THE DOUBT. I am generous with myself, allotting myself a piece of the pie. Maybe I even give myself the first piece. Wouldn't that be radical! No more putting myself at the back of the line, subsisting on the leftovers of my energy and consideration. My well-being enters the equation. I count too.

⊕ ⊕ ⊕ ⊕ ⊕

*How will I show myself
that I count today?*

*In what ways have I put
myself last?*

*What would it look like to be more
generous with myself?*

⊕ ⊕ ⊕ ⊕ ⊕

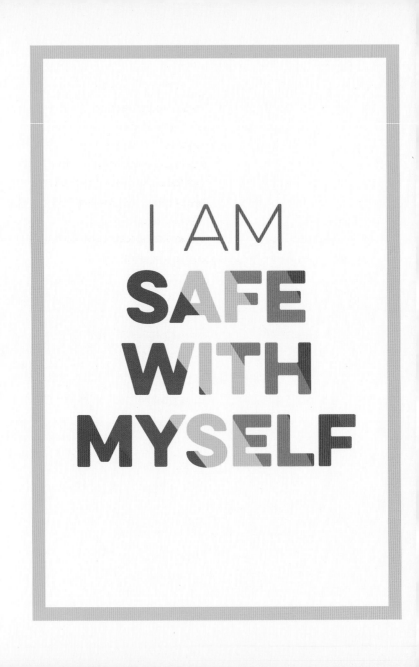

I AM MY OWN SAFE PERSON. I can turn to myself at any time for comfort, protection, and security. I have my well-being at heart. Inside is a safe zone where I will not be thrashed, attacked, or criticized. I can relax in my own self, in my own body. I am the guardian of this inner world and am vigilant about whose words and energy I let in. I am a peaceful warrior protecting my boundaries. I surround myself with people who have my best interest at heart and who are gentle and kind. I make choices that make me feel secure. I take measures to relax my nervous system so that I can feel how safe I really am inside myself.

* * * * *

Can I be gentler with and more protective of myself today?

Do I peacefully and vigorously protect my boundaries?

What measures can I take to be safer in my own self, in my own life?

* * * * *

I AM
INTUITIVE

I HAVE AN INNER VOICE THAT IS WISE, KNOWING, AND ALWAYS AVAILABLE TO ME. I don't know why I know the things I do, but I just do. I trust my gut. I listen to the warning bells that start ringing inside, at times out of the blue. My intuition guides me to say yes or no. The more I listen to it, the louder it speaks to me. I let it guide me in matters big and small. If I suddenly get a hunch that I must turn right, then by all means I do. My intuition permits me to avoid danger and to go toward windfalls. My instincts are sharp, and I am deeply connected to them.

⁕ ⁕ ⁕ ⁕ ⁕

Will I check in with my inner voice today?

How do I become quiet so I can hear my intuition?

How has my intuition served me in the past?

⁕ ⁕ ⁕ ⁕ ⁕

I REACH
HIGHER

I CHOOSE TO ELEVATE MYSELF. I raise my vibration by thinking about the goodness and goodwill in my life. My positive attitude and my focus on love enable me to rise. I am inspired and encouraged. I climb out of whatever hole or situation has kept me down. Everything I do is in service of keeping my energy high and vibrant. I make careful media choices. I spend time with people who are positive and kind, and stay clear of those who deflate me. When I feel my energy drop, I bring it back up. As I raise the level at which I live my life, it enables others to do the same. There is a whole new world that exists at a high vibration and I'm going up to meet it.

* * * * *

What can I do to rise today?

*Are there people in my life who
make me feel deflated?*

Who encourages and inspires me?

* * * * *

I GUARD
MY PRIVACY

MY TRUST AND THE PRIVILEGE TO BE LET IN ON MY CONFIDENCES ARE EARNED. I decide who enters the inner circle of my world. I take care of my personal life. I don't owe anyone explanations. It's not a question of keeping secrets; it's a matter of preciously guarding my privacy. While I happily take part in social and community life, there's a whole other part of me that is off-limits and by invitation only. I owe myself that special, safe space for exploration, self-discovery, and rest. I can always come home to me.

* * * * *

*Am I clear on what's private
and what's public for me?*

How do I honor my private life?

*What aspects of my life are
by invitation only?*

* * * * *

EVERY DAY I PUT MORE HEALTH INTO MYSELF.
I make choices that enhance my well-being because it is my highest priority. I am willing to do what it takes to feel my best. I give myself the greatest chances for the greatest health with the self-care I provide and the expert care and information I seek. I support restoration and balance with my favorite healing modalities. I believe in the amazing power of my body, mind, and spirit to recuperate, adapt, and grow. I show gratitude for all the parts of me that are strong.

* * * * *

Will this—what I'm about to eat, do, or say—enhance my health?

What will I do today to foster more health in myself?

What parts of me are healthy and strong?

* * * * *

I WELCOME
CHANGE

LIFE IS INTRINSICALLY ABOUT CHANGE. Every living organism and ecosystem is in a constant state of flux, and I am no different. I don't turn my back on life by trying to keep everything stuck in time and futilely resisting change. I'm not the person I was before, and tomorrow I'll be a new version of myself. I am flexible and have an incredible ability to adapt. I am constantly learning, growing, and transforming into a stronger and truer self. I am at peace with the new.

* * * * *

*In what ways am I changing
right now?*

*How have I transformed
in the past year?*

*Do I resist change, or am I excited
by what is possible?*

* * * * *

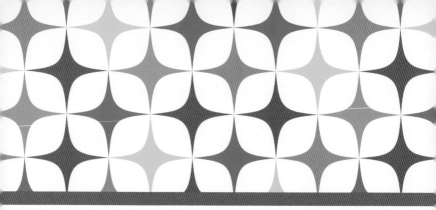

I HONOR
ALL MY
EMOTIONS

IT IS SAFE AND BENEFICIAL FOR ME TO FEEL MY FEELINGS. I trust my emotions as they communicate intelligence about me and the world around me. Each emotion carries a message, and I take time to understand it. I feel, therefore I know. I don't suppress my feelings. I let them flow in and out of me. Sometimes they are fierce and other times subtle, and they encompass the whole range, from deep grief to lighthearted joy. All of them are acceptable. I won't be gaslighted into believing I don't feel what I feel. Some of my strong emotions, like anger, can even provide energy and leverage to make big changes. I find skillful and healthy ways to get in touch with my feelings and to express them when beneficial.

● ● ● ● ●

What are three emotions
that I feel today?

Are there some emotions that I won't
allow myself to feel?

Do I need help to trust and
feel my emotions?

● ● ● ● ●

I AM
BOLD

I'M UP FOR ADVENTURE AND TAKING BOLD FIRST STEPS INTO THE FUTURE. I expect the unexpected in myself and in my life. I am comfortable with the unknown. In fact, I delight in the remarkable that pops up in my life, my heart, and my mind. I usher in the new. The past does not determine my future. I know that good surprises are in store for me, and I reach for them—no matter how far they pull me outside of my comfort zone. I cannot be boxed in.

* * * * *

*What can I do to seize
this new day?*

Do I let myself be unpredictable?

*What new future do I boldly
want to step toward?*

* * * * *

I AM
CURIOUS

I DON'T PRETEND TO HAVE ALL THE ANSWERS.
I remain questioning with an open mind and an open heart. I don't jump to conclusions and immediately judge. Instead, I stay present with my curiosity and with my questions. I'm interested and inquisitive. Let's see what happens. Let's see how it works itself out. Let's see what will be needed. Sometimes there's nothing for me to do about a situation. I just remain curious about it. I wait for clarity and answers to come in their own good time, and I trust they will.

* * * * *

*What situation do I face
right now that can benefit from
more curiosity?*

What answers am I awaiting?

*Can I refrain from jumping
to conclusions?*

* * * * *

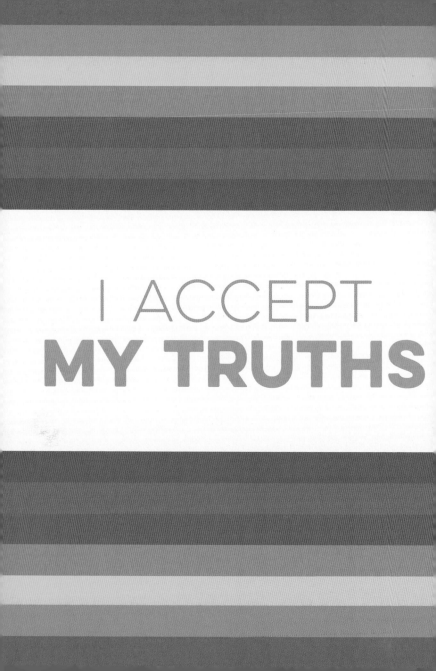

I ACCEPT
MY TRUTHS

I ACCEPT MYSELF JUST THE WAY I AM, AND MY LIFE JUST THE WAY IT IS. I don't live in denial with my head buried in the sand. I look at what I know to be the truth—even if I don't like it or it makes me wince. I recognize and acknowledge it for what it is while still striving for my highest potential. I walk with ease that exquisite fine line between acceptance and knowing that more is possible.

· · · · ·

What has been difficult for me to accept?

What would it look like to fully accept myself?

Can I walk that fine line between acceptance and seeking my highest and greatest good?

· · · · ·

I AM
FREE TO
BE ME

I AM INHERENTLY FREE NO MATTER HOW THE WORLD IS UNFOLDING AROUND ME. Freedom is my birthright. I have the freedom to make the very best of every circumstance. I am free to decide how I show up and how I behave. I choose what I think, how I feel, and what inner words I use. I am free to dream and shoot for greatness. It's within my power to decide what I value. My heart is mine. My spirit is mine. My body is mine. My love is mine to give.

· · · · ·

Do I see myself as inherently free no matter the circumstances?

Which of my freedoms is most important to me?

What is in my power to choose today?

· · · · ·

TO BE NICE IS TO BE AGREEABLE AND POLITE, TO TREAT PEOPLE WELL ON THE SURFACE. That's different from kindness—allowing genuine care to drive behavior. My intention is to be kind while still staying true to who I am. My thoughts, words, and actions are benevolent and always within the realm of choices available to me. I am a force for goodness in this world. My humanity and compassion are an integral part of who I am. I choose to be kind even when it's not easy, even when I have been triggered.

⬤ ⬤ ⬤ ⬤ ⬤

*How will I show my kindness
toward others today?*

*How can I be kinder
to myself?*

*How can I show kindness in
moments when I am triggered or
with difficult people?*

⬤ ⬤ ⬤ ⬤ ⬤

I
CULTIVATE
**A RICH
INNER
LIFE**

MY INNER LIFE IS SACRED AND IMPORTANT TO ME. There's a lot going on underneath the surface. It's in this depth that I make sense of the visible and invisible worlds. It's where I define who I am. I have dreams and aspirations that begin and bloom in this space. So much vies for my attention in the outer world that I make it a point to go inside where I can feel my emotions and decide upon meaning. I am happy when I am committed to and connected with the deepest, most personal part of myself.

● ● ● ● ●

What can I do today to enrich my inner life?

What does having an inner life mean to me?

Do I long for more opportunities to turn inward?

● ● ● ● ●

I AM
ORIGINAL

I DON'T NEED TO STRIVE FOR ORIGINALITY.
There has never been anyone exactly like me on earth and there will never be again. All I need to do is to be myself and to be at peace with who I am. In fact, originality is the stripping away of the beliefs I've accumulated that aren't true to me. It is releasing what doesn't belong to me so that I can be distinctively me. Instead of asking if what I do is *good* enough, I now ask if it is *me* enough. All that I create is as original as I am when I do it my way and follow my vision.

* * * * *

*How will I honor my true
nature today?*

What do I want to create?

*Are there any beliefs I can release
that no longer serve me?*

* * * * *

I AM
A SEEKER

I AM AN ENTHUSIASTIC STUDENT IN THE SCHOOL OF LIFE. I am on a path of self-discovery. I wonder about the universe and my place in it. I am a spiritual seeker, questioning and looking for evidence of a greater purpose and truth beyond everyday life. I have an intense desire for spiritual growth and for a meaningful connection with the sacred in and all around me. I follow in the footsteps of pilgrims and mystics, a tradition as old as humankind itself.

● ● ● ● ●

What do I most question today?

How dedicated am I to my path of self-discovery?

How much do I occupy myself with spiritual matters?

● ● ● ● ●

I AM
SELF-
CONFIDENT

I VIEW MYSELF IN A BRIGHTLY POSITIVE WAY.
I am sure-footed and confident that I can figure things out. I am self-assured. I know what my abilities and skills are. I have faced many obstacles in my life and have survived. In fact, I've thrived. I am talented, accomplished, and experienced. I am capable of being the highest version of myself. I don't base my life on what others think. I have trust in my own mind that will take me as far as I want to go.

● ● ● ● ●

What do I feel self-confident about?

What areas of my life could benefit from more self-confidence?

What are some of my abilities and skills?

● ● ● ● ●

I EAT
MINDFULLY

I GO FOR NOURISHMENT. I CHOOSE FOODS THAT KEEP ME STRONG AND HEALTHY. I eat slowly, with mindfulness, noticing and taking pleasure in every bite. Eating well is an intrinsic part of who I am. I lovingly prepare good food for myself. The food I eat is delectable with high nutritional value that gives me energy. When I find myself eating out of habit or to stuff down an emotion, I stop and take a few deep breaths. Then I ask myself: What would bring me comfort? What do I really need at this moment? I feed myself like I would someone precious to me.

· · · · ·

What foods would bring me pleasure and nourishment today?

Am I eating mindfully, noticing and enjoying what I eat?

When I'm feeling stressed, what can I do instead of eating?

· · · · ·

I AM
THOUGHTFUL

I PUT CONSIDERATION INTO WHAT I DO. I am thoughtful of myself, my loved ones, my home, and my community. I tread lightly on our magnificent planet. My thoughtfulness increases our mutual well-being. It brings joy and healing and demonstrates that I care. I anticipate what may be needed or desired. This shows people they are seen and not alone. I ask myself how I can make life just a little better for myself and those around me as I go through my day.

· · · · ·

*How can I make life just
a little better today?*

*Is there someone in my life who
is struggling and would benefit from
an act of thoughtfulness?*

*How am I being considerate
within my community and the
world at large?*

· · · · ·

I CONNECT
WITH
COMMUNITY

I ENJOY CONNECTING WITH PEOPLE TO SHARE INTERESTS, SPACE, FELLOWSHIP, PRACTICES, AND BELIEFS. Our bonds enable us to move forward together with strength and ease. We keep one another going. I eagerly participate in my communities in all kinds of ways. I want the group spirit to be vibrant. I love being in a community of like-minded and like-hearted individuals committed to the same cause, creative endeavor, or spiritual pursuit. Community is a remedy for loneliness. I belong to the people in my communities; we are connected. The more I give to my communities, the more I get in return.

● ● ● ● ●

*Which communities are
dear to me?*

*How do I contribute to
my communities?*

*Am I interested in
creating a new offering that would
benefit the group?*

● ● ● ● ●

I AM A
VISIONARY

I CAN SEE THE GLORIOUS POSSIBILITIES OF LIFE.
I spot openings, answers, and prospects where others
see problems. I am amazed at my ability to see the
unseen and bring it to life. I visualize how I desire to
be and how I desire to live. I envision my future as one
I am totally in love with. I see the absolute best version
of myself up ahead calling to me. The future in my
mind's eye is bright and bursting with life. I hold a big,
bold vision of the greatest potential and I rise to meet
it. My insight, imagination, and creative capacity to
dream a life into being are limitless.

* * * * *

*What's my vision for
this new day?*

*What glorious possibilities do
I see in my future?*

*What is something that is apparent
to me but not to others?*

* * * * *

HUMOR HAS A DELIGHTFUL WAY OF UPLIFTING ME AND RAISING MY ENERGY. I empower myself with my sense of humor. I use levity in all kinds of life situations. Once I find a way to laugh with kindness in the face of drama and negativity, they loosen their hold over me. Laughter increases all my feel-good hormones and relaxes me. I look for opportunities to be silly and amusing, and I cherish friends who crack me up. I am thankful each time I laugh.

· · · · ·

*Am I facing a situation
right now that would benefit
from a little levity?*

*Which friends of mine
make me laugh?*

*Can I tap into humor even more
to raise my energy?*

· · · · ·

I LET
OTHERS BE

I AM NOT HERE TO CONTROL AND MICROMANAGE OTHER PEOPLE, OR TO SAVE THEM FROM THEMSELVES. I recognize and respect that we are all our own beings with our own feelings, dreams, and lives. I allow others to learn their own life lessons without interference. I love them freely and take delight in them just as they are. I know we are all on our individual paths doing things at our own speed. I joyfully focus on managing what is mine, and let others do their thing.

* * * * *

*Am I trying to micromanage
someone else's life?*

*What would it be like to let others
make their own calls?*

*How will I focus on my
own life today?*

* * * * *

I AM
SATISFIED

THERE IS NOTHING MORE TIRESOME THAN BEING WITH SOMEONE WHO CANNOT BE SATISFIED.
I refuse to be that way. I consciously decide to find satisfaction with myself and my own efforts. They are good enough. I am good enough. I do my best and relax. I will not live my life second-guessing or living in hindsight. At the end of the day, I am assured that I am loved and that I'm doing fine. Even while I continue to bloom and reach, I also appreciate myself just as I am right now. I choose satisfaction and fulfillment, seeing every little victory and learning and remembering what is good and what works in my life as opposed to what isn't or doesn't.

* * * * *

What is going well in my life today?

Am I generally satisfied with myself and with my life?

What brings me true satisfaction?

* * * * *

I PAUSE TO
CELEBRATE

I TAKE TIME TO CELEBRATE LIFE'S BIG AND SMALL MILESTONES. I commemorate my achievements and those of my loved ones. Celebration acknowledges the preciousness of life and all the gifts it has to offer. It is a pause in the busyness and a chance to lighten up. I can celebrate with grand ceremonies with others or in the quiet of my own heart. Either way, celebration acknowledges what is important in life and how capable I am. Plus, it's so much fun!

* * * * *

*Do I celebrate my achievements
and milestones?*

*When was the last time
I celebrated?*

*Can I take a few moments
today to commemorate something
that is important to me?*

* * * * *

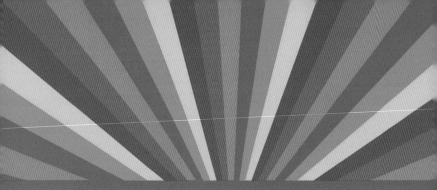

I HAVE
REVERENCE
FOR MYSELF

I LOOK UPON MYSELF IN ADMIRATION, AND ACT IN WAYS THAT REFLECT THAT. I live within my own standards and have integrity. I am excited to be me. There are things I just won't do, places I won't go, and people I won't spend time with because they are not in alignment with me. I have too much self-love to break my bond with myself by turning a blind eye to what is not in my best interest. I am devoted to myself. Devotion means that I don't forsake myself or pretend to be someone else. I speak in my genuine voice, expressing my own truths. I am steadfast in my allegiance. I am loyal to my own calling, mission, and vocation and do all I can to fulfill them. I am the object of my own loving dedication.

* * * * *

How can I show myself more reverence today?

Do I express my authentic truths even when it's not easy?

If I were completely loyal to myself, what would I be doing or not doing?

* * * * *

I AM
DELIBERATE

WHATEVER I BRING MY ATTENTION TO GROWS AND GETS ENERGIZED. My focus is so powerful that I must use it carefully. I consciously bring my attention to what I want in life and who I want to be. I deliberately choose to place my focus on positive creation. Want more love? I focus on that. Want more abundance? That's where my attention goes. I don't let others drag me down in their drama. I choose not to ruminate about negativity, saving my energy to target all the positivity and joy available.

. . . . .

*What do I specifically want
to focus on today?*

*Is there anything that I don't
want in my life that I have been
giving my energy to?*

*Where are my attention and
energy best focused?*

. . . . .

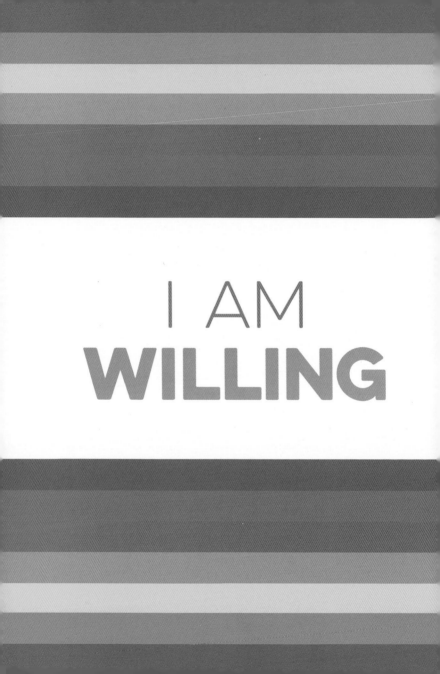

I AM
WILLING

I HAVE AN ASTONISHING LIFE FORCE INSIDE ME.
My determination is limitless. I am excited about both my life now and my future ahead. When opportunity calls, I eagerly answer with a resounding yes. I go for new adventures with great enthusiasm, jumping in with both feet and my whole heart. A passion for living overflows in me—so much so that others are drawn to me and my spark ignites sparks in their lives as well. I am willing to do whatever it takes to follow my own calling. I'm all in, ready to go where my spirit takes me.

* * * * *

*What am I enthusiastically
happy to do today?*

What am I passionate about?

*What am I willing to do to create
the future that I envision?*

* * * * *

I AM
DISCERNING

NOT ALL PEOPLE OR SITUATIONS ARE A GOOD FIT FOR ME. That's just the way life is. I don't need to forcefully make anything fit—to appease myself or anyone else. I use my perceptiveness to know what is in my highest good. It's not a matter of judgment or thinking I'm better than others. It's a realization that my time and resources are finite, and I choose to use them wisely. My insight and instinct guide me. Knowing how to discern what is right for me is a skill I cultivate.

● ● ● ● ●

How will I use discernment today?

*What is in my highest good
and interest right now?*

What feels right?

● ● ● ● ●

I AM
SENSUAL

I HAVE A POTENT SENSUALITY THAT I ENJOY INDULGING. I recognize the need to get out of my head and to give my senses free rein to lead me to new experiences and awakenings. My sensual nature is timeless and always present, waiting to be tapped into. I am aware of the energy that flows through me, making my skin tingle. I want to play, be light and free. I let my body feel good and move in its own natural rhythm. I take time to listen to the desires of my heart and delight my senses.

● ● ● ● ●

How will I enjoy my sensual nature today?

What feels good to me?

What makes me want to play?

● ● ● ● ●

I AM
AN ALLY

WHAT I BELIEVE AND DO MAKES A DIFFERENCE.
I have the power to make my life and this world a better place. I align myself with just causes and virtuous people. I use my energy to advance them. You can count on me to have your back. Together we increase our strength and make a significant impact. My contribution is essential to our collective well-being. My participation counts in whatever way I decide to join and lend a helping hand.

⚬ ⚬ ⚬ ⚬ ⚬

*Whom or what will I ally
myself with today?*

*Do I see my contribution as essential
to creating a new world?*

*Who are my allies in
my own life?*

⚬ ⚬ ⚬ ⚬ ⚬

BEING LOVING IS THE MOST VALUABLE AND TRANSFORMATIVE CONTRIBUTION I CAN MAKE TO THIS WORLD. Love is always enough. I keep close to my heart loved ones, cherished objects, precious memories, and my own self. The more love I give, the more I receive. How fortunate I am to care so deeply. I spend time every day thinking about all that I love in my life. As I do, my heart expands, becoming stronger and radiating even more love. This inexhaustible source of power is me.

* * * * *

How will I show my love
to others today?

Whom do I keep close
to my heart?

How has my love been
transformative?

* * * * *

I AM
ON A
JOURNEY

NOT ALL THOSE WHO WANDER ARE LOST. It's a classic truth I bring to my life. My life isn't just about meeting goals and arriving at a set destination. What may look like a dead end can actually be a crucial detour where I gather wisdom, valuable skills, and new friends. I let the journey unfold as it wants to, even as I set my sights on somewhere. Who I am and how I handle the challenges and windfalls of my journey are what count. I may reach some milestones and I may not. That takes nothing away from the value of the grand voyage of my life.

*　　*　　*　　*　　*

Do I acknowledge how far I've come in my own personal journey?

What have I gained from the detours I have taken?

Do I enjoy the process even if it feels like I have so much to do?

*　　*　　*　　*　　*

MEET THE
AUTHOR

MARYSE CARDIN is dedicated to speaking to herself with love, humor, and kindness, and to helping others learn to do the same. She is the author of the books *Speaking to Yourself with Love*, *Speaking to Yourself with Love Workbook*, *Self Talk Love for Sensitives*, and *Self Talk Love for Fertility*. As a speaker, workshop leader, and university communication teacher, she is passionate about sharing positive, loving self-talk skills. Maryse is driven by her desire for everyone to have lives filled with love, health, calm, joy, and fulfillment. She believes the right inner conversations can make that happen. You can continue the morning magic with Maryse at selftalklove.com.